APOSTROPHES IV: speaking you is holiness

APOSTROPHES IV

speaking you is holiness

E.D. Blodgett

The University of Alberta Press

Published by
The University of Alberta Press
Ring House 2
Edmonton, Alberta T6G 2E1

Copyright © E.D. Blodgett 2000
A volume in (cuRRents), an interdisciplinary series.
Jonathan Hart, series editor.
5 4 3 2 1

Canadian Cataloguing in Publication Data

Blodgett, E. D. (Edward Dickinson), 1935–
   Apostrophes IV

   ISBN 0-88864-352-7

   I. Title.
PS8553.L56A764 2000   C811'.54   C00-910461-5
PR9199.3.B54A884 2000

All rights reserved.
No part of this publication may be produced, stored in a retrieval system, or transmitted in any form or by any means, electronic, mechanical, photocopying, recording, or otherwise, without the prior permission of the copyright owner.

Printed and bound in Canada by Friesens, Altona, Manitoba.
∞ Printed on acid-free paper.

The University of Alberta Press gratefully acknowledges the support received for its program from the Canada Council for the Arts. The Press also acknowledges the financial support of the Government of Canada through the Book Publishing Industry Development Program for its publishing activities.

Apostrophes IV: speaking you is holiness is published for the book trade.

Das Du ist älter als Ich, das Du ist heilig gesprochen.
—FRIEDRICH NIETSZCHE

Tibi

Contents

1 Mother
2 Child
3 Emerging
4 Epithalamium
5 Baptism
6 Credo
7 Afternoons
8 Polarities
9 Redemption
10 Noon
11 We
12 Stone
13 Evenings
14 Spirit
15 Gods
16 Bhakti
17 Genesis
18 Rose
19 Words
21 Sea
22 Stars
23 Pneuma
24 Fire
25 Earth
26 Seed
27 Remembered
28 Lakes
29 Flower
30 Empyrean
31 Fireflies
32 Quest
33 Leaving
34 Dreams
35 Sung
36 Response
37 Rivers
38 Sequentia
39 Anagoge
40 Apples
41 Autumn
42 Roses
43 Imago
44 Prayers
45 Tending
46 Ground
47 Menorah
48 Now
49 Shadows
50 Bare
51 Evocation
52 Alone
53 Orient
54 Mirrors
55 Open
56 Horizon
57 Grandeur
58 Rain
59 Green
60 Voices
61 Going
62 Finding
63 Idea
64 Stripped
65 Pictures
66 Together
67 Brevities

Our mother was the moon. No past belongs to us except the night,
and when we were in our childhood, we must have been a pair
of moons, but smaller, underneath the stars, the sky spread out upon
our backs, and what we knew of ourselves was what we knew of how
the moon appeared, the time we kept a breathing of the turning months,
before and after but a respiration, all our history there.
The twilight is a flesh that we put on, but twilight where the birds
are turning grandly over nests that they have placed in us, a flesh

that has no final shape, its sight uncertain in the trees. The snow
at dusk descends through us, the colour that reflects from it is blue,
a blue that reaches everywhere along the snow until it seems
the way infinity might look among the trees. We turn upon
each other then, the measures that we make a meeting of the light
against the snow and blue it adumbrates. The memory of us
in our childhood is a possession of the snow, the moon
upon it. No one holds it, but its silence is in us—it is

what we would have as bones—its silence and its passage through our flesh,
but we have held the sky in its unbearable fragility,
the sky that was a childhood of moons and stars and nights that are
what turn in us. Your breath upon me is a breath of what we were
beneath the stars. If we saw it, we would see that childhood
is blue, the shadows on the evening snow, and giving back the light
the moon bestowed upon it, shades that seem almost mythologies
that carry other moons within themselves, and us in our birth.

Mother

We have mothered us. It is the rose that flowers in our mouth
and speaks, the moon that rises from our hands upon our body, light
at play within our eyes, a light where animals would move, the fates
that bind them now released. Children were playing on a shore, the sea
drawn up against their feet that dance upon it turned to birds, their cries
gone up into the skies and calling back to them, and all of them
as one look up to see if they are there. Their silence looks at them,
the silence of the light upon their flesh, the silence of their eyes,

the silence of their feet across the shore. No one will say to us
who we might have been before, nor do the words for saying it
belong to us, but in us there are letters lying everywhere
and in between them silence, our silence, our letters. We
must be a space where children in amazement take their place.
We lie in silence, spelling now the moon and later roses in
our body—: seas come up, the birds lie low upon them, traces of
their play a light that flowers us, and our our given up.

Child

The flesh that covers us is elemental, it recalls the wind
that comes across the sea with birds aloft in it and each one
a bird that sounds the space it fills, a wind of distant flowers, none
known to us—but elemental: of the air alone and sea,
and of the earth that we have held within our hands, of fire that
upholds our bones, anatomies of fire setting us within
the moon's sphere where nothing we have seen is not revealed to us

in its infinities, the moon an open rose of magnitudes
where we have gazed upon ourselves at play within the night, a rose
of you and me in our dispersal in the light. Your hand upon
my face is but the moon when it is new, its newness now the flesh
we share, and stars appear beside it, our stars, the space that is
of our possession unconcluded—space of birds among
the stars, an ancient fire sheathing them, and of the sea beneath,

the stars among the waves. We looked into the night, its depth unclear
to our eyes: are we, when we are one, the night we thought we saw,
the moon upon our flesh, its light our skin, the stars in flight,
encircling our bones? Your face appears to me, unknown within
the night of our flesh, the rose of our revelation. When
it opens, silence opens with it. We are in the silence, night
the only sounds that we exchange, the moon emerging from our mouth.

Emerging

Somewhere in eternity it snows, a snow suspended in
the air without wind. No one could tell if it were snow or stars
as dense as thickly falling snow that never reached the ground, a snow
where planets came and went, the sun was seen to move among them. You
are standing side by side within the snow, eternity spread out
upon your backs, the taste of it within your mouths, unable to
distinguish snow and stars. Perhaps the stars will rise between you, when

they come at night, and not as stars but words that have no meaning you
have known, and words that are not of an alphabet that spells the trees,
the stones and falling of the light that you have seen before, but words
that open in the air, the music that they make of stars and snow,
a heaven opening within the words and rising from your mouths,
mortality forgotten. Never were you so alone and one,
seeing what you are composed of stars in their infinitives,

the possible of snow apocalyptic in your eyes. You are
not you, but origins of music, music made of syllables
that speaks to nothing, *fiat lux* its only score, the stars the one
antiphonal. Divinity is song, a universe the words you speak,
nothing now your breath where stars and snow appear about you. You
can do nothing now, your movements not your own, the light that speaks
speaking you, where solitudes of stars unutterable rise.

Epithalamium

A bird stood up upon my heart and sang. The silence afterward came down
about us, a new rain of silence in the air. This was no rain
that Adam knew, and Eve beside him in the garden, walking through
their cloudless spring, apple trees in flower, rain that fell for them
to see silence on their naked flesh, but our rain that lies
upon the grass is that garden of our knowledge, apple trees
of silence rising up between us, silence the horizon that

embraces us. Can there be birds of silence only, birds
that are the singing mind of silence, birds who sing and in their song
the grass stands up in answer, small stones that lie beside the sea,
each a moon for other suns? Our hands within the rain
are spilling over, fountains of the silence we have brought to place
before each other, music we remember poised within it, its
imperatives the guise that our flesh puts on, of rain and grass.

Baptism

When I read you now, the colour of the moon is elegiac.
Night has come upon you slowly, auras of it moving round
your feet, unnoticed in the grass, solemnities of moon and night
that fall, the one place of their insistence where you are, and all
that you can gather of yourself is in your breath. You say it was
the moon that breathed, the night in its recesses audible within
the air, a breath that moves in larger measures, breathing for the grass,

a dance of the invisible that dances on a stone all by
itself, an offering of grass, the earth breathing green, the night
within its darkness open, stones and grass, their strophes breath. To be
is choral: what we are is not of us but in the giving up
of grass as it becomes assumed in night, the dance of smallest stones
with what they cannot see, unknowing where they are within the passing
of the moon upon their surfaces, no other credo theirs.

Credo

Throughout the fullness of the afternoon you gathered roses. Later they
were placed within a vase, and in the twilight of the room the smell
of roses settled in the air about us. Gestures that we made
were made with roses held in mind, of roses opening within the light
we gave to them. We may forever stand within this light, as we have stood
within the length of afternoons, the flesh that sits upon our bones
a more transparent flesh where roses in the summer pass. Your face

and mine would flower in the later afternoons, the vase of earth
supporting us, our bones within the longer light grown gnostic, each
initiate of dances known to roses, summer and the rise
of evening over us. If we are gathered, we shall gather us,
the rose of our body open where the afternoon comes down,
and it will enter us, as roses once have entered us, and where
it moves will be the dance that our bones in their auroras are.

Afternoons

The body that we are in darkness dwells. The blindness of the night
inhabits it, and we, our flesh awake, are dispossessed of skies
and other distances, proximities alone within our grasp,
the nearest stone, the grass, the wind upon our body when it wills.
We are not where we are to find. As if we were become a tree
that is its weathers, what we know unbidden is the rising in
us of us waking. Shapes of roses and the moon is where we are—:

we cannot move without their transience upon our flesh. What is
this gift that we have given us, a rose in summer and the moon
within the night that enters us but gifts of what we are to be?
What we are cannot occur in any other moment than
the now of roses opening invisible in our flesh,
and when they open, we are known, an orient for them and star
that rises in their north, a universe beside it going round.

Polarities

We lay in bed for months. A small economy grew up around
us. Were there birds, they would believe us, marking their positions in
the air with our bodies, smaller animals would know that death
was not to lie upon our hands, our breathing but an astrolabe.
We may have reached the place where there were only sighs, nothing yet
to see, the place of murmurs, eloquence of sound to no end
that we would know. To touch transforms the flesh possessing us, our skin

incantatory. Time is our becoming: our rising is
the rising of the stars, the fire that will be their being ours.
When we hear it, we will be the birds that turn upon us, trees
that gather shadows, wavering of moons, and in this universe
where are you and I to lie, the you and I of us without
the certainty of bone? We are a you and I that are of no
remembering, the wind within us, revolutions of the stars.

Redemption

Perhaps we are unknown to flowers, roses opening within
rosarias of space, nothing known to them but passages
of bees, the entrance of the sun into their hearts of roses, time
unreckoned there, the time of still waters at noon, where vapours of
the sun emerge, morning and the evening star invisible
within the firmaments of memory. And if the rose should take
thought, its study would be moments of its distillation in
the sweetness of the air: it is the rose and not the rose, its time

entelechy unmeasured, summer's major air, the music of
it what it knows, and silence what it is left unknown. The silence of
the rose is our space, our sun and our moon contained
within its breath, breathing what we know. To speak for roses we
exhale the words, not knowing what they mean, innuendos of
their fragrance plashing on our flesh. The rose is where forever is,
and in the summum of its summer, music through its gardens moves,
the silence of our flesh its song, its noon the knowing of the rose.

Noon

The nights are growing longer. Rains will come and fall about us, rains
that come from summers we remember. It will not be rains we hear,
but their dimensions in the air will be the world we hear, the nights
grown longer on our flesh, the sound of roses opening within
our ears, the grass against our skin, their intimations pressed upon
us, bodies we had thought our own now of summers and of rain,
of nights where our darkness flowers, no more capable against

the rain than any stone. Waiting grows inside us, a destiny
of longer nights, of two asleep upon the sky at home among
the stars attending us, other roses, impossibilities
of shade dispersed into their light. To be born is not to fall
alone across infinities, the sun a solitude of fire,
the body of its burning closed. The rain is ours, we the rain's,
and we may turn to snow and lie upon our summers, spread upon

the grass, our raininess abandoned. We are walking in the rain,
the hands that touch the hands the rain bestows—: then a birth is known.
It flows upon the flesh we thought was ours, and we are in the rain,
the rain in us. Summers are not a memory, summers are what
we are and our capability, the we attending you
and me. If we had flesh in that then when we took flower in
the air, it would be summer for the moment worn, ours for the sun.

Horses were walking slowly through their high autumns, fields going
out of sight. It seemed as if the sun were lost, and where we stood
was in its loss, the light dispersed around us. The slightest stone that lay
beneath our feet was our orient. Wherever we would walk,
we turned to see it there, the sun upon it and the rain. And if
we dreamt, we dreamt of its inevitable place, of horses in
their dreams of autumns passing through. The stone we saw was not ours,

nor anything we dreamt of where it was, sufficient only as
a mark upon the ground. This is where an autumn rises known
to us, beginning of a knowledge when the sun does not traverse
our bodies in the night. What it knows is where the silence is
that is our gravity, the moon that holds the dream of our flesh
suspended, horses moving in it and their autumns. Radiance
is all that we can hear. It rises in us naked in the night.

Stone

Only the evening moved about us, its arrival not to be
perceived among the trees but where their shade was spread upon a wall,
the figure of it tending through the air and drawing wall and tree
within the reach of evening, nothing touching, yet their being was
the making of that space where evening gathered shades upon our skin
as we entered it, a gate against a cosmos drawn apart.
Where is the ground of sense, the common, where the children tumbled from
the sky exchange upon their darkened breath silent icons of

unchanging orders of the seasons in their immortality,
of fruit forever full and heavy in the sun, the ground where elms
undying sweep the sky, the smiles of the children primal and
of no desire? Where? The landscapes that are ours do not lie
so languidly before us—: their imperfections are of moments in
a twilight rising in us where the trees are cast in shade, and when
they move, the murmur that we hear is one that does not always stop
for us, nor is the fruit they bear unmoved against the sun which when

it turns goes round and round an absence that it cannot reach. Know
that what we know does not give up whatever it may be wholly
to touch. Something escapes—: the branches of the trees a shade against
a wall, unable to resist the motion of the evenings that are without
forgetting, evenings ruminating in their leaves, their leaves content
in us, spread open on our skin, the evening that you are a place
without the measure of finality. An emptiness is in
our flesh, an emptiness of twilights and a leaf suspended—there.

Evenings

Horses were standing in their wests. The sun within its distances
was laid upon their flesh. They bore the sun without a sound except
for breath as a response, the great fire that they know an air
of patience measureless and grand—: impossible for us to see
the sun and not to comprehend the breath that horses make. But what
of roses, moon and motions of the trees, all within their wests,
the wind upon the hills? We are west for you and me, the sun
that we possess coming and going on the breath we breathe upon

our flesh, the trees beside the lakes reflecting every turn the air
makes. When our flesh is one, it is not known whose mouth upon
it moves, or whose the sun that sets upon it, setting on the hills
that stand against the edge of our sight. The mind is then a tree,
the motions of the wind within its leaves the deepest knowing it
attains, my knowing you a breath where roses rise, later moons.
We fear the end of breathing, knowing that the mind would reach an end
and at the end we would not hear the sound of horses there as they

transmute the sun, unmindful of the trees where our thought, the thought
that is of you and me, conceives whatever is that dwells in us,
a wind that passes through the leaves and then is still. Then we are
breathless, knowing the air in us, our air, that is the rose
that stands suddenly in us and sings the rose we are, our breath
alchemical and standing on horizons of the sun, the moon within
the western sky a moon of our exhalation, opening
in our passing near the sky, and us in flower for the sun.

Spirit

Destiny might have made us gods, the sun for us forever in
its zenith, trees that stand about us not dependent on the change
of season, never growing fuller in the late largesse of one
more summer's day, the beauty of our bodies radiant against
the sun, almost invisible from all the light. As lovers we
would be exemplars, each of us a mirror in each other's hand.
There is no harvest for the gods. The fruit that hangs upon the trees
is of mortality, mementos of their passing pleasures. We

would bathe in roses, petals flowing over our undying flesh,
roses incapable of withering away, and standing in
the fullness of our knowledge we would speak in words of absolute
precision, aphorisms falling from our mouths into the sun.
Embracing our bodies in the mirror of hands, we would
not long to see ourselves without illusion, one in flesh and mind,
our food the sun alone, the logos of it our sustenance.
Your eyes would be the gaze of pure ideas upon my face, their light

the sun's. We would not know of anything that comes and goes, the moon
within its mysteries would not caress our flesh, and no desire in
our hands would move with sadness toward the provocations of the rose—:
no movement would be ours, the stillness of the noon embrace enough.
You would be my clarity. We could not speak of anything
eternal, knowing but perfection. We would be exemplars of
an end, and we would love, the lightness of our hearts undisturbed,
the beauty of the rose upon us nowhere flawed with gravity.

Gods

I want to be the world asleep inside you. Darkness would
be our place, impossible to know the nearness of the things we knew—
certain trees, the earth against our feet—except our flesh in its
complicity, and sleep across us falling, a sleep of slow snow.
Time for us would be the darkness that we have become, the one when
the when of our flesh impassioned in its sleep, a sleep that dreams
of us who were the sea inside itself before it was the sea.
Before beginnings were, divinity lay down within itself

and slept, unable to do more than dream of its divinity,
itself apparent to itself, no other way to be known:
its dogma was the rose, the light of summer passing through itself
but visible as a divinity in flower. Of ourselves
what other knowledge may we have, of light that we have taken in
our sleep, that rises in the dream of our flesh? No other than
as our flower are we to see ourself. It opens in the dark.
No other moon is ours rising up in flower from the sea.

Bhakti

We never see our faces. Sometimes we are given images
of ourselves reversed as in a mirror or of something like
ourselves in passages that float on water, our faces but
faces that are blue, composed of shafts of grass when we are close
to shore and barely visible within the sun. But when we face
each other, eye to eye, the nakedness of our flesh appears
to disappear, our faces given back, the face that I had known

divined unseen in yours, and all about us darkness fits itself
to us, nothing to see but our eyes in their exchange. The dark
cannot be parted from our sight, it is what we have taken on our flesh
to be our nearest knowledge. So we know by our laying on
of hands, our faces now at our fingertips, the darkness that
we offer to the world blest. Without the sun hypothesis
would not be known, but everywhere the world would take shape within

our hands, not resting till the seventh day, the waters parting, day
and night moving on our bodies then, the only skin that we
are given, paradise proximity, and air invisible
when birds sheathe us in song, the animals of our knowledge beasts
enfolded in our darkness. What would we possess beyond the dark
that gathers us, the sound of our breathing azimuth enough
for us, the music of it grass, the filiation of the trees?

Genesis

We sat beneath a row of poplar trees, the shadows of their leaves
playing on a stream that lapped against our feet. They formed a skin
upon the stream, dappled moments of the dark that held the sun
apart, a sudden brightness when the wind moved where sand appears
and rocks beneath the surface of the stream. We cannot escape
the presence of the sun—: the shadows on the stream are ours and
the stream's. There is no sun that enters us, our darkness undisturbed,

the sun without a setting there. We do not live in time, but sit
beneath a row of poplar trees, and in us taking shape a rose
in our darkness absolute stands up. Its petals move, the dark
around it yields minutely, petals of a rose immeasurable
that in their motion have no place to go but merely open and
in their opening to spread the dark apart, until the dark
appears a rose. The moon makes no ellipse against the rose, the stars

too far, floating forever in the sky, but our darkness, not
remembered by the closing of the light, the darkness given us,
wakens, a darkness knowing nothing but the open, not a rose
but what the rose in its perfection is, and in the open we,
as if a stream exposed were at our feet, open, our dark
displaying its becoming rose. Now we have no place, we are
unmeasured, moving farther outward, shaping air, replacing suns.

Rose

Where do they go, the words we speak, the words that settle on our breath,
shaping the course of our exhalations, trees that rise before
our eyes, their branches thick with leaves, the sound of birds unseen within
them, or the melody that they invoke and then are gone no sooner
than their notes are heard, or someone's face remembered passing through
the dark? We speak ourselves, the words about us rising in the night
as we lie down beside each other, our ears intent upon the sounds
we make. We know that all of us is there in syllables, that what

we said when we began to talk is in us as an echo, but
an echo only heard in what we say in this moment, a voice
that speaks from somewhere in our flesh and going back to it, the air
we breathe and our flesh in their desire making us: it is
a rose that opens in our ears, our flesh open. But is it flesh,
this place where animals within the darkness stand, their breathing ours?
I hear you speak them, and all of them are animals of no name,
but passages of their being moving into ours, the sun

upon them, blessing them without sound, the sun within our words,
making time for us as we converse, the setting sun of our
horizon. When we sleep, silence covers us, spread upon
the flesh we think is ours. What it is is not disclosed to us,
unnameable as any animal we know, a silence of
the moon that dwells within it and in our words, a gift we make
in our making us, shaping the moon and rose of silence. We
are born in silence, words remember us, and so the rose that stands

unspeaking in my hand is us in our unknowing of the what
we are becoming, axis of the words we want to say. The rose
is nothing more than what we want to be, its gift a giving up,
the fragrance of its silence overcoming us. Our birth is not
forgetting, it assumes the silence of our flesh, the silence of
the dark, the moon, the animals within us. Silence opens, we
open. When we speak, simulacra of our knowing rise
in us. They take the shape of roses and the knowledge roses are.

When I woke, it was not skin I felt upon my body. Night
had fallen over me, I wore the dark. Now the moon might rise
within me. None would see it, but its rising would become the shape
my body has. You lay beside me sleeping, the one sound your breath.
If we are anywhere, this is our geography, an air
that is the score of our flesh, an annotation spelling us.
I do not think that it was you beside me—: it seemed to me a sound

that was arising from a sea, and I invisible was lying
in the dark beside it, the sea exhaling waves. If the gods
were anymore, they would not stoop to speech, but we, when they were in
their ecstasies, would leap into the air, spilling over from
their mouths, sufficient words for them to name an order of the world.
So you would become the sea, a sea of sacred utterance,
and I the hearing of the sea, its answer to the moon in me.

Sea

The trees were motionless beside us, stars were sliding through the sky.
Somewhere in the dark a bird cried out, and silence fell upon
our faces. We stood within an air that rose from trees, and our light
was light the stars had shed. We heard the dark, the silence could be touched.
There is no other place for us to be, and what we know is here
in its beginning, standing where the stars have given up their light.
Contingency was overcome, a random cry at night. It seemed

that in our knowing we became eternal, breathing with the trees,
taken in by silence and the stars. But even stars fall,
no trace of them for us to find within the sky, the light of stars
that we had known growing dimmer at our feet. Our stars
are stars that are for moments in the sky. Our stars are where
we are. They rise at night in our darkness. Trees are visible
within their light, and birds in their occasions cry below the dark.

Stars

These are landscapes where the footing is unsure beneath our feet.
Not everything is plain before our eyes, but all the flowers that
we see are blue. Perhaps the fragrance of the roses here is blue,
their presence what we breathe. I touch your face. Your skin is not within
my hands, but something of the sky, memories of the moon, the sun
diurnal coming back. How am I to think you mortal now,
the bright antiquities of flowers, blue, and moons reflecting on

your face? We live as flowers live, the blue of their unfolding in
our bones. When I hold you, bones are not in my possession, nor
the flesh where you seem manifest. But what are flowers, grass, the slow
departure of the summer afternoons, and are we not within
their passage, moving into our autumns? Moons must die, and suns
fall in ashes through the universe. But flowers open when
their flowering is full, and something in the air is changed. What are

these roses, then, we hold within our hands, our faces touched, the sense
of bones beneath our fingers? Flowers are our gift, we give ourselves,
an offering of flowers in their absolute fragility,
a gift of our mortality that we give up. We are not we
when this occurs, nor flowers, nor the vagaries of light across
the sky, but open in the lateness of the year, a fragrance that
we cannot name possessing us, and when we breathe we breathe ourselves.

Pneuma

We stood unmoving in the sun, and from a distance we could not
be seen, no shadows falling from our bodies to the ground. The flesh
that was a barrier between us fell away. I called your name
and heard the word anatomize, the letters leaping up, the flames
that they became the you that I desired on my tongue. The are
of what we are is not the dance of flesh but flesh that is the light
that falls upon the tree, the blade of grass, the stone, and each is us

in analogue, the matter of us momentarily transformed.
What is my speaking you but our dissolution in the fire,
the sun that enters us the summons of our stoniness? It is
the light of us at our prayers saying: come with me and bid
farewell to bone and flesh, the shadows that we cast of bodies not
our own. Our body speaks the sun, our flesh its albas. Light is what
we hear, not words, the dance of our tongue upon the fire poised.

Fire

Sometimes we saw the trees were not as we had thought. They were the earth,
its yearning to be of the air, and in the silence that spread down
upon us, we could hear the earth, the breathing of it in the nights
of summer, breathing stars, the passage of the moon. We are trees
that walk, the slow andantes of the earth moving up against
our feet. The stars are not above us, they are burning in the breath
of earth, and so the moon, antiphonal of all desire, holds

us, tree and earth and air, as one flower open in the night,
a flower of the silence taking music's shape, the trees no more
discernible than air. We are the reaching of the earth, its breath
in us the rose of our body more than rose, a gravity
that is not ours but the turning of the earth in us, a dance
not ours but ours in a music of the earth, the time we keep
not sun but moon, its rising the geography of our flesh.

Earth

Both of us had seen the trees, the grass, the adumbrations of
the sun among them. We saw they were not us but were horizons for
us where we walked, sometimes green and sometimes bare, obeisant to
the changing sun. If I am finally only seed, and you the ground
in which I fall, we have given ourselves to grass, the green
breath of earth. How shall I know that you are not what I shall be,
the grass of us of one condition? I must have been asleep,

else I had known in that moment given up to grass that I
was not the flesh that I remembered but a place where flowers sprang
upward to the light, my body ground enough, or flowers are
my sleep and you my waking. Now birds grow up inside us, the sun
that sleeps beneath their wings the sun that circulates in us. We do
not see the trees, the air of their exhaling our exercise.
The gift that we exchange is green. When we speak, our breath is leaf.

Seed

Before we were the we we are, what were we, you and I? A stone
there is lies farthest from the road exposed upon the ground, the sun
upon it, the rain, the wind, vulnerable in its inmost cell, the stone
that no one saw, and it composed a universe, its stoniness
its being, no more to do but be, centuries marking it. But you
and I were not, before, of any time. The skin that both of us
possessed was our mortality as you and I. We wore away

and watched the sunsets pass. One day in the evening one of us
and then the other disappeared, both of us forgotten. If
there is a memory, it's we who are the memory. Sometimes
we will speak of you and I who come upon us by surprise,
and something like us will take shape in our stories, each of us
emerging from mortality again, and other sunsets passing. We
are our deathlessness, the present of us our naked noon.

Remembered

Lakes at the end of summer cast their dreams into the august air.
Standing near, where trees run down to water, we can see ourselves
go up towards the sun, being dreamt as lakes would dream, birds
gathering within us, following the sun. We are no more
but gazers on ourselves within a dream of summer in the length
of its imponderable rising upward, what it was unknown
among the images of birds and trees and us. Alchemy

and anagoge is what we are. It is not words that we exchange
within the light's supremacy, but you and I as aspects of
the sun, the summer and the lake. Silence, then, is not the air
that moves around the sound of what we say, it is the saying. When
we move in our dance above the lake, the gestures that we make
make of silence music, and the music is what we become,
but music visible, the sun upon the lake, mirage to hear.

Lakes

The flowers that we held in our hands we gave each other. Both
began to flower, seasons shaped around them. Spring was briefest in
its passing, showers falling, preludes of the summer sun that seemed
to be unmoving in the sky that hovered over them. We thought
they were a mouth where heavens entered, planets lingered, and the moon
for them appeared another flower overhead, amorphous in
the evening sky. The galaxy that found its way to them could not

have been much larger than the space of spring and summer in their breath,
the constellations fully formed and resonant with flower myths.
The soil that they stood in was a soil made of our hands,
no difference we could see between our fingers and their roots, the rain
that falls on them our rain. In our garden moons do not
go up into the sky, they are an invocation of the light
enfolding us, flowers breathing soundlessly, the passion of

the stars in our breath. Of all the silence we can know, we are
an origin for it—: as if a moon it rises from the ground
of our flesh, the air between us air that flowers offer. Words
are not what we are given. Bees might enter us, and what we think
is us they carry off, dispersing anything that we might say
farther in the sky, our silence falling through mythologies,
our immortality a dream of opening that flowers dream.

Flower

Side by side we lay, the ground beneath our heads, and open to
the sky. Sometimes there was rain, and it would fall upon our skin,
and we would know the rain. The sun passed over us, and we would not
ask why. If we had any orient where we would turn, it was
toward the moon. It was a light that seemed to breathe above us, all
the light inside the night becoming spherical and then into the stars
exhaled, their breath upon our flesh a second skin. Time for us

descends, falling from the stars in their eternities, and when
the thought of them takes shape, the thought that rises from the ground beneath
our heads is formed into a rose that spoken opens with our lips.
It is eternity that opens there, the guise of it no more
than what a summer can possess, but summer in its plenitudes,
the breath of summers falling one upon the other entering
the rose that is the we of our falling open underneath

the moon. The rose is our breath. It does not know the past: it is
and then is not, its winters our inhalation. Stars descend.
They fall in us, another sky and ether. We are ground for their
inseminations, sown with light, the our of us rising up
as stars would rise on their horizons, punctual upon the dark,
the roses of our thinking empyreal over us. What is
is fire, our being roses flaming open in our mouths.

Empyrean

When I was young, the summer passed upon its distant porches, slow
summers, but infinite in their dispersals, no one believing they
might end, the air illuminated momentarily with small
incursions that were thought to be the stars, but stars against a sky
that any child standing near would comprehend, and from above,
from porches dimly seen within the summer nights, blessings fell
from time to time. You might have thought that these were signs that fell

from some divinity on us, assurances that were the sounds
of voices, not the words, a music in the summer nights that with
the floating stars was all there was to know of heavens, earth
and other mysteries. Sometimes those stars, forgotten porches, rise
upon the mind's horizons, sudden voices enter its régime
of darkness. Paradise is what it seems, a dance untamed among
the stars, but in your absence nights of memory without a moon.

Fireflies

Trees when seen beyond the windows always seem larger, more
of trees than if the windows did not interpose. We are not sure
if what we see, whether the air that rests upon their leaves, a light
longing to be green, a sun refusing to be sphere, a sun
at play, has any basis in the ground. The holy wood is not
displaced in glass. The trees take root in us, and animals go forth
from our bodies, the chiaroscuro of the light not light or shade

but genesis at genesis, not the sun but the summons of
the sun, and in that light the animals are born. There is no glass
against that light, the sun immediate upon their flesh. They are
the light in shade without a memory of void, and for the trees
there is no language—: this upward issue is a prayer uttered by
the air. Our being with the trees is an efflatus, wind
in passing, leaving us, animal and sun and tree sent forth.

Quest

I saw you walking through the room and out into a hall. The air
was undisturbed. Your eyes alone remained behind, and they were birds
so small that they were barely visible in flight along the walls.
Then they were gone, and through the windows leaves were audible. It was
another autumn coming down, the moon at rest upon its huge
horizons, night grown more intangible. It is not certain now
that it was you who brought this passage in the room, autumnal breaths,

the dissolution of the birds, or if it were but solitudes
descending through your bones. This is not death, not birds in flight, not rooms.
It is an aspect of the air that bears upon the flesh, a fate
more intimate. Nor was it you that passed—: it is the way the air
is our memory, saying what there is of us to say,
that we are rooms, the brevity of doorways, chairs where they are placed,
the moonlight falling through the leaves a stay of their mortality.

Leaving

Dreams in their dispersal are unable to depart, they cling
to us with the small hands of souls that fear abandonment to wind
and rain, exposed to stars alone, that when the dawn will come, there will
be nothing left of them but spaces in our memory, the light
of every star put out, the trees of their reconnaissance, the grass
becoming dimmer in their sight, until there is no more to see
but what we have forgotten, scattered through the places stars have left

falling into night. We are our dreams and through the lengths
of darkness touch each other with uncertain hands, seeking stars
that fall unknown between our fingers, dreams that blindly flutter up
and down our flesh. Memory is memory of us, the dream
of our possession that has laid its hands upon us, its embrace
what we have woken into. Stars come out, the grass is risen in
it. Animals of our acquaintance leap into its nights, their breath

in us. We are not born of flesh but of the memory of dreams
that lie awake in our dark. No other age is ours but
the age that water has or stars, their everness the stuff that fills
our bones, our anatomy ubiquitous unto the songs
of birds that steep the summer nights, our anatomy the night,
the summer, and the air of dreams that is our skin embracing us—:
we dream ourselves into our birth, the moons of our memory.

Dreams

We woke to song. It was not birds we heard, it was the world, its
ineffable now uttered, music in suspension in its breath,
and birds ubiquitous within the early air, the music of
the world flowing through their mouths. Before that instant, they possessed
no more of being than their flesh, its sleep and silence. Being sung,
the air leaps naked up against our bodies, brushing us with its
uncovered breath, the world given up to us. Before us trees

were not the trees, no grass or flower rose corporeal before
our eyes, but they were sung, and what they were was drawn against our skin,
the world taking shape in music on our flesh. We are the air
the world sheds, our nakedness an absolute, opening
as we awaken. We are song. The world is not where we are,
we are where the world is. The moon does not come up within
our eyes, the meaning of it mere measures our flesh assumes.

Sung

Your book lay open on a chair beside me, its pages strewn with shades
of young leaves. From time to time the wind moved among the leaves,
the patterns that they made amorphous, neither light nor shade, but their
contingencies at play, and there we seemed to sit together *en
famille* beside a river speaking of whatever came to mind
and disappeared, our syllables becoming birds that rose into
the air until there was no difference between our speaking and

the sky. Let us say the mind is a tree and each branch a pure
hypothesis that opens underneath a purer sun. The wind
that moves within it comes from music that comes suddenly to mind,
a breath that is scored on still water, willows tracing on
it propositions that would lay the world bare, a world of
forgotten things that pass beneath the sun, things that are of no
epiphany, things we might see as instants, only themselves, things

that are of music in an infinite transfiguration, moon
that is not moon but our voices in their music singing its
fugacity. Mortality is how the moon appears, a moon
in variations, floating on the water, an idea that
suffuses through the leaves, and yet a moon in palingenesis
that we have never seen before that when we speak takes shape before
our eyes, floating upward from the mind at home among the stars.

Response

Rivers in their slow solemnities lie down beside us, they
and not the air the place where our flesh appears to end, rivers
taking thought upon their infinite beginnings, rains against
sobrieties of mountains, brief freshets in the wind, a glaze
upon the rocks, and everywhere they gather in the emptiness
we thought lay next to us, of air and its unfathomable blue.
We had been asleep until this moment in the air, our
belief that we were creatures of the discourse of the sun and its

diurnal ordering of air, but rivers in the silence come,
their sole expression an amphibious afflatus—: willows appear,
rising on their flanks, their waters breathing with the dreams of fish
and grass. The rivers we take up into the hollows of our hands
are our shape, our bodies willow shade, the light that glistens on
our flesh a light of water in its passage. Rivers are the thought
that circulates between our hands, and we are islands, trees within

their seasons rising in our words. We do not live for endings. If
we are to gather form against another's eye, our edges would
appear invisible, merest whispers somewhere in the dark,
bodies immersed within the meditation of their offices,
our hands upon our flesh within a fall of music. Suns for us
possess no nostalgia, the longing that we know contained
in one touch, our movements dances of the rivers through our bones.

Rivers

It could have happened in another way, but that moment when we
arrived, the air before us broke, and in the broken air there was
a sparrow singing on a fence. All around him clouds stood back,
the great sun itself forbore. It was not light or shade that held
us in that moment, nor the bird in its fragility, it was
the song that burst upon us, raining music through us, touching that
of us that we are sure is everlasting, where we and music in

the darkest dark remain. No bird there is that overcomes its brief
occurrences—: it lives in consequence, the flowing after of
its song that spills upon the wind, its air the air that lies within
the grass, the air that enters us. The moment that we think we live
is afterward, a then of now when one song is in us in
its flower rising in the rain. No other silence at the end
of music falls. Where are the moments then of our being in

the music? Where are sparrows, rain, the dark, the spilling music that
we heard, the grass, the wind? The moment of its happening was all
at once, no other sparrow known to us in its intransigence,
sparrow, song and flower an event that was the one event
that was, but in its being being other than it was. What is
is not, the consequences of the sparrow not the song but that
eternity we thought we were before its song fell over us.

Sequentia

If there is nothing we possess, then our bodies are the last
of our possessions. We for us are our occasions, the body that
you grant to mine is mine when mine is yours, both of us possessed
when wholly dispossessed, and we are no one then, lying in
each other's arms, the music that would enter you a music that
enters me. Who is it then that gazes at the world, arms
against the window sill, looking through the air, who sees the trees

where they are standing in the light, trees that stood before they rose
upon the eyes, solitary in the sun, their branches bearing
seasons? Let us say that it is us where shadows fall, the weight
of seasons, sun and leaves remembered infinitesimal upon
our flesh, but flesh that now is not ours but abandoned where
we lay, the trees above us our now, the seasons moving them
moving us, the temporalities of summers our embrace.

Anagoge

Falling through the autumn nights we heard the apples loosened from
the trees. It was their final passage, slow nocturnal music rising
from a ground of grass. It was how destiny might sound, the rhythms
that it kept incapable of steady order, going nowhere but toward
the ground of its beginnings. When they meet the grass, the silence they
preserve throughout the summer breaks, no more audible than flowers
in the wind, and we begin a dream of dancers dancing over

sand, a dance that cannot keep the pace of sun and spheres, but moves
unthinking of a centre, its only time occasions of the sand
and foot, the dance epitomized, a dream of the invisible
across an endless shore. The dance inhabits us, and we for us
are gifts of apples, the music of their brief adagios against
the ground music of an infinite punctuality that we
are measured by, the dance that dances us, of apples, grass and night.

Apples

It seems that nothing here has ever moved, and distance stands upon
its dim horizons waiting for the world to begin to turn
into itself, its completions manifest. Nearest things—
the grass, the flowers that surrounded you, the surest knowledge we
possessed—they are all within their distances withdrawn. Your hands
appear invisible, and if we know them, it is music that
we know them as, similitudes of something toward the evening

that rises up against the sky, music without cadence that
can be heard but barely where your hands had been—: it reaches out
to gather stars that flower farther in the air. The music is
of old injunctions just beyond our ken, a murmur of the gods
among the leaves that hands us to each other, icon and gravure
of music that is us in its embrace, the distance we perceive
a gathering in us of evensongs forgotten given back.

Autumn

We are each other's rose. You stand in me as I in you. The earth
is not where we have walked before, the grass familiar at our feet,
the sun an orient for us to find the trees, the rivers in
their passage, orders of the stars. We cannot find the knowing of
our hands, the air uncertain on our flesh. It settles into us,
our only scripture its uncomprehended dance that takes its place
in us. We are the open where it moves. Nothing that we do

is what we do. We are done, and we in our being rose—:
the sun is not for us to see, it enters us within the air,
the light of temporality the rose we are, the memory
we have a memory of roses absolute, the summer the
unchanging locus of our grasp upon the dance of air, the change
of night and day unknown to us. We are the breath that we exchange,
its strophes turning round upon our mouths, returning us to us.

Roses

On occasion in the night your face appears in silhouette
to me. It is your face in effigy, I thought, that I might see
but dare not touch, premonitory in its outline, all alone
and holding up the air that lay upon us. Nothing in the room
had changed, and yet the space that it contained made me think of trees
when they are old, and I could breathe the majesty that they exhaled.
I have read that elsewhere in the world, birds in their designs

are not the birds we think they are, but gifts that are conferred on us.
There were no birds within the room, only the memories of trees
spreading their roots in us whose seasons are uncounted in the end,
and only you and I, and images of dreams that come and go
among didactic trees. This was not sleep where we have been, nor can
we wake to our familiarities again, the birds that we
have known or trees, and words that I would choose to speak to you are now

not clear to me. Flesh cannot be what we are, nor can the things
that lie about us in this room respond to what we say they are.
They are in their simplicity the signs of some imperative
that we bestow upon ourselves, exchanging breath throughout the night
within the room where we have been. But what we are is so to be
unable, given to trees and traceries of birds. It is enough
that we have known the sun, the passages of night, the shape of breath.

Imago

As others say their prayers, we would tell each other stories in
the dark, and they would reach around us till within their arms we fell
asleep. We spoke of us as flesh and its becoming word, the light
that enters us the light of our speaking, bones that gather in
the fire dancing through the quick economy of our breath,
the voices of our body turning through itself. We spoke of you
and me, both of us persona of ourself, this trinity

that we surrender to our words. It seems that when we speak that we
are born of silence, our origin an exhalation of
the you and me that are suspended in our mouths. We did not learn
this anywhere but here, the language that we know a speech of flesh,
the dark, the breath where we are shaped. Silence wraps around us when
we fall asleep, no other memory of us to be heard. We sleep
inside ourself, our birth a breath away, asleep upon our tongues.

Prayers

Roses stood against the window. On the other side the snow
lay down upon the ground: it had done what it was going to do,
nothing but being white was left. There was no movement anywhere—
only the moon that came upon the snow, impossible to tell
what white was of the snow or moon, or if it was the moon that moved
or the dark that followed it and edged away. Roses the
unmovable, the air surrounding you refusing to depart,

flowers that suspend whatever we would see of stars, the turn
of constellations, planets slipping into night and silence, o
the ground that lies beneath our feet, it rests upon the open rose,
our terra firma, irrevocable apodosis,
a sentence where the words are roses, roses that we do not see
but roses speaking: moons in what they say are moons that sing of seas
beneath the southern skies, interminable moons that more than moons

become the summa of the fullest moons, the seas the great refrains
of what they sing. When we are spoken, it is in a sentence filled
with moons, the open sea, another cosmos standing up, the grass
in us. We have no where: the order of our being spoken, an
orient already that is us in its possession, *there*
are roses, roses that emerge unseen from roses. If we are,
it is in our tendency, our being being, then, toward.

Tending

Let us say that roses open, then we are. Eden, then,
is our rose, the one forbidden is for us to be the rose,
our only knowledge knowledge of a place, and in that place
the music of the birds, the leaves that flutter on the trees, the stones
that in the streams are taken out of silence—this is not us but where
we are when we are uttered, you and I, in naked syntax. If
we ask, our question is desire of the rose, and we and stones,

the breathing moon are what is asked. The rose's tongue is who we are,
and we are signs of revelation which the rose would speak. Were you
and I not we, the real of roses would be roses that are in
their winters white and silent, landscapes that do not assume the shape
of any sentence, where you might fall at random through the air, or stones,
nothing of our anatomy to know in its remembered sequences,
intimacies of ground, the grass that played upon the senses gone.

Ground

All that our body dreams is what we are. And so a tree grew up
inside us—seasons lie beside it, snow and leaf in counterpoint
against the light through seasons where the turning wheel of birds in space
would pass. It is a tree whose crown contains the rose of sun and stars
spread open through its branches, a tree of our desire where
the dawn upon the sky expands, a snow of light from somewhere in
the galaxies suspended. Seasons breathe: the breath that passes through
them—shadows of the birds its only darkness—our breath

that is the rose in flower, sun and stars but consonants that are
for us a gravity, the measure of our body's dream. The flesh
we wear is what we are when we are spoken, seasons spread upon
us, silence and the shade our punctuation. If to live is to
be born, it is to be a word in time, but time perpetual,
a tree that, in its always leaf and seed and branch, its body in
its genesis a *fiat* rooted in the breath of our flesh
within its dreaming, is of our earth that bodies forth in air.

Menorah

Now there is no now but where the newly risen moon is on
your face. I put away the past I knew and, heedless of a life
hereafter, I make this oblation to the moon incarnate where
descending it makes light of your mortality, the heaven of
the sky upon my fingertips, and all the seas come one by one
to fall against your feet until you are an island of the light,
the seas emerging from a universe, the sound they make beyond

what we can hear, seas whose knowledge is no other than to give
obeisance to the moon, and what we thought we heard was every sea
giving way as you begin to fill the heaven of the air
around us. Planets are our only family now, the sun a fire that
is kin to our fire: how are we to walk again upon
the earth, unable but to gather it into the light that now
is what we are, the splendour of the grass inside us and the stones?

Now

Could it be, you asked, the dead have dreams, and could it be that in
their narrow spaces nightmares rise of dreams of their mortality
or do they dream when they lie down as if to sleep that they are dreams
that we might have when we embrace at night, the dead alive in us,
our dreams a dream of palingenesis, the moment when we wake
the moment when the dead are dead? Graves are what we carry in
the sun, the silence that they make the shadows that we see beside

us, motes of dust that stand against the summer. If the night, the moon
alive again is where the dead make overtures to us, and we
are theirs, what when we are dead will be of us, or are you now
the dream of what I dream, already taking me into a dream
of immortality, and I inside your dreaming you? Then we
would be our dream, a dream of our waking, waking into one
enfolding shadow that we cast about us, its light the dreaming moon.

Shadows

Antiquities of trees are standing everywhere beside us, leaves
absorbed into another time, their silence old. We touch the stones
that lie against their roots, our hands grown naked, bare eternity
upon our skin, the nearest we might be to stars. We lie within
the night that falls around us and nocturnal air that bears the moon,
the centuries of space. We speak, and words come slowly from our mouths,
the language we exchange within the silence indecipherable,
but words that we can see, assuming shapes of things that are unknown

to us, accustomed to the trees, the stones, the we we are in its
primal, the air that hangs upon the words we utter absolute,
you and I forgotten. We are we without the qualities
of age, the night the flesh that makes us to each other clear, the moon
our breath, the only gift we have the naked now that we have placed
upon us, nothing to remember. Silence holds us, silences
of stars around us, the knowledge they possess what we at play put on.

Bare

My father's hands were hands of an austere beauty—ships might sink between
them, falling through the deeper seas, and they would not have heard the sighs,
other finalities that spread beneath the waves, the haunted fish,
his hands unused to music. Cats he loved, and they approached him as
a friend, their eyes a silence luminous against the air. They left,
gathering all the silence in their disappearing bodies, moons
departing. The beauty of his hands did not touch, it opened space

where nothing, taking its occasions, entered, constellations of
the stars, the moments of the light, making darkness manifest.
I call you, father, now to enter spaces that were not within
your grasp, the silence that conjoins but momentarily the space
between a phrase of music and another, or a word and then
a word to follow, ships emerging from the seas, a melody
unknown around us, beauty without mortality between our hands.

Evocation

I think of you alone, and in my thoughts there is no landscape that
appears, no tree, no sky, no place where you might enter. Shadows fall
without light. I cannot see your face, and where your eyes might be
distances of music come and go, a music that cannot
be seen, but if it were, your eyes would find it, sorrow rising as
a smoke against horizons in the winter rises, sky and smoke
uncertain in the air, the motion that they make a motion that

your body knows, and you, adagios of solitude the scene
where you are placed, are music that I cannot hear. My hands upon
the circle of your flesh are given music—greater weight the grass
would not possess, if it were lying there, or smoke, or winter sky—
a bowl of music, then, where shadows are in their descent how we
appear to us descending through an evening air, our gravity
without assertion, shadows of a music passing through itself.

Alone

Sometimes I find myself alone and standing in your room. Upon
my skin a second skin of light lies down. I cannot recognize
myself inside the light, dissolved among the other objects filled
with that unmoving light we share, a light containing chair and bed,
a light that in its settlement appears to be but hardly here,
its true possession birds in passage through a forest where the leaves
have fallen to the ground where you were sitting once, the sun upon
the river glancing at your face, and in the air between the birds

and you the images of what you dreamt rose up and disappeared
into the light that is of you. The place where I am standing is
nowhere but in a light of vanished birds, forgotten dreams, the sun
in autumn falling. I am not a place, nor you. Moments of
a light that comes upon us, light that has no source within the air
is our where, our bodies bright with temporalities. When we
inhabit us, it is not flesh that we possess, our bodies in
the light, but emanations of what we are almost yet to be.

Where we are is where we are when our bodies are the time
that we are giving up, a rain that fell without my knowing it
through afternoons that were of me when I was young is now a rain
that lies upon your hands, a rain that is of radiance itself
spread open in the air, and we are standing in that rain and in
an afternoon that is an afternoon where our knowing us
is knowledge of the rain and our standing as we are within
the rain, a rain that is of that that our bodies turn toward.

Orient

We made our way across the field until we reached a lake, and there
we saw the grass had changed, the willow small. The water touched our feet.
We gazed upon the water, seeing we were lying there, our hands
entwined. Our bodies rose and fell, yielding to the movement of
the water, broken intermittently, the fragments of our shades
dancing together and apart upon the water. We waved at us
and we waved back. When we stopped, we saw that we were still, the lake
alone in motion. We saw that we were sleeping open-eyed, the light
in them no brighter than the light upon our bodies. Everywhere we are

this simulacrum of ourselves is at our feet or in the air
of windows through the rainy afternoons, no being possible
without its being there, an underworld always at our feet,
submissive, us in mime, as much of us as of the water, sun,
the glass and air. We cannot say exactly who we are, but where
we are is somewhere floating in the elements, reminding us
of where we are when we lie down to sleep, unprotected and
together with our shade, ourselves shared and bedded down within
the dark that rises at our feet, the grass of our flesh in flower.

Mirrors

Where we stood the world lay open. No beginning was behind
us, moments we might say possessed a shape where we could find a way
to some more distant parent time that we might mirror to ourselves.
Our knowledge is of now. The words we might have heard, if there had been
befores for us, would stand upon our tongues unspoken till they were
forgotten, words without the syllables to give the open to
our sense, our mirror us. And so I look at you and you return
my look with yours, our looking meeting where we are, open and

without a bearing in the space we make. The silence of our looking
is for us the primal silence. What we know in origin
is there. Were we to breathe into this now, our breath would be the breath
of roses, their unfolding our looking on each other, both
of us within our eyes, no other time for us but this exchange
of breath. The open is the open rose of our gaze that can
not see the open or its breath. We think we see, when we are seen,
our invisibility the world open opening us.

Open

The horizon where we sat was not well known to us. The sun
fell in foreign ways among the trees. We were unsure of how
we might compose a world, our presence there a temporary rest.
Certainties of things that we had known were placed upon the ground
in front of us, one horizon slipping past another, stones
that we had brought from somewhere else, tokens of some other place
that we had known when we were not where we are now. You placed a stone
into my hand, a stone that would configure others into shape,

yet when it stood in that horizon, it began to open. This
is not a stone, you said, it is what I have been and cannot be
again. It speaks through me but keeps what it has been in silence, so
it seems to be a stone. Rivers run through it that we will not know.
Beside the rivers, voices speak that I have heard of people who are now
not alive, so I must speak for it, all their voices flowing
into mine. When you spoke, a darkness lay about us, your eyes
withdrawn into the solitudes of rivers that have passed, of stones

that keep their silences. But it was not a stone. It opened in
the close horizon of my hand. It must have been a flower that
your speaking had evoked, a flower where the frozen country of
your childhood lies still inviolate and open only in
a voice that murmurs in the dark falling on the stone that rests
open in my hand, where all dark begins to open in the space
we are, a darkness no more visible than we, the flower then
horizons flowered, our darkness this petalled universe.

Horizon

When she died, the tutelary trees that stood around her house,
their early summer grandeur come again, exhaled upon her no
more power than the air they breathe, their beauty theirs. You and I
remain, forgotten in the moment of her going, and sit here
where the dark is darkest, trees and flowers left outside. You spoke of her
in those countries where you had been with her, and of her beauty and
the power that she had, my hand in yours. Around us in the room
were traces of her presence, nothing that could not be held within our hands,
remnants, perhaps, of a great feast that are forgotten in the dark,

but each of them you proffered to my sight, breathing on them brief
resuscitations of that beauty gone and power. Grandeur dies
in fragments, nothing left for us to do but grasp at it and call
its name. No more than words is our possession and the breath that shapes
them—: there is her eternal rest, the fragments of each word you spoke
recomposing her eternally. Now she is of many
things, her trees and flowers and familiar fragrance. Grandeur dies
and we are here within the rest of it, its darkness on our hands.

Grandeur

Through a night of rain the earth exhaled its breath in us, the shape
of flowers rising open in us, flowers of invisible
departures, bees exploding into novas, fractions of the light
falling, a fall of rain unheard, falling through our flesh. If
we were to touch the light, the bright illumination of the grass
that stands against the flowers in their open rising, bones that turn
within their summer's passage briefly into that rose that we
beneath the rain become, our touch would be of moments, grass of green

nows to trace upon the rose of our body. When we touch,
our hands in their ephemeralities abandon touch, nothing
that they know inside them, only the breathing earth, everywhere
within us, holding us unfolded in the rain. All that we
can be is in this moment, trajectories of bees almost
beginning, almost ending, open, yet to move, between, a dance
arrested, nights of rain that you might think to grasp—but breath, it moves
without our seeing it, the earth upon its breath, it moves in us.

Rain

The prayers that we speak are green, the colour of the sea when it
is near, prayers of easy waves where fish and other creatures are
at play, a paradise without the interruptions of the mind
awake—it is a leaf that opens in the sun or music of
apples falling through the autumn nights, the grass alone awake
with sighs—and through the nights we are at prayer side by side, too dark
to see ourselves as temporary things of flesh, but knowing we

are everywhere about us, even in the farthest stone, our tongues
at play forever giving birth, a world taking shape upon
them, and see, we are there within the garden, walking where the first tree
takes root, the birds surprising us with fire through the air, the dogs
sitting near the edges in their dreams. In our prayers we
do not have names, enough to be the green when it is spoken—: we
are our prayers walking on our tongues, the sea upon our breath.

Green

The windows fill with voices of the children floating up upon
the small waves of twilight playing through the curtains, waves that dance
without thought across the lakes of evening lighter than the air
that breathes them into being, waves of air and fragile music that
possesses them. How do we know that we are overhearing who
we were, before we knew who we became, not you and me, nor us,
but voices that were the air of summer, what the summer sang

when it rose up within the grass, of children filled with airs that are
all that they can be, the summer taking voice in them? It can
not be a season, then, for they are summer and its passage through
them. Summer is a breath, but breath that is the air, the trees become
a music that when it descends into our flesh is what we hear
of green, and so we take ourselves into ourselves, our summers known
upon the breath of children floating over us, and what we know

is music falling over us in twilight, fragile, green and of
the motion that comes over lakes beneath the passing air. We are
in this possession then, music that is not what we have heard,
but music that is of our knowing, music of the mind that is
the dance we are when we are given to the early dark, our breath
in us a singing of children in their possession of the air
that passes round the stars, the summer lifting off above the lakes.

Voices

People are walking down a street. The moon above them is a stone
in flower barely open in the twilight after rain. A dog
is running at their side, people walking along a street beneath
the trees and moon, and when they pass the window's edge from where we watch,
there is an emptiness that follows them that has the look of chairs
steadfast within their solitudes so firm you might have touched it. They
are gone, the trees and moon remain and something in the air, and we

are still within the room, a moon within our eyes. If trees could move,
they might have followed, disappearing past the window where the light
grows dim. We have the moon. It opens in us slowly till it begins
to move into itself again, flower after flower that
return to their invisible beginnings, emptied of the moon
they are. It is the shape of us that breathing gives, an emptiness
that is in us the flower that is ours after moons are gone.

Going

A tree stood up inside us. Mirrors of the leaves broke open in
the sun, and each of them began to burn. So there is where the sky
would find itself if it were lost, uncounted suns and moons upon
its branches turning. Birds within their light were speaking syllables
unknown to us into the burning air, enigmas that were signs
the sun and moon translated, each of them responding in their place
within the air, none without the other moving, all attuned
to music that appeared to spring from where the birds were sitting in
the tree, the music in them folding open from the air. It is

not song but something in the silence where the music that they tell
that is what they in singing are, not music nor the sun and moon
that are the syntax of their sound, but of the tree, its fire and
the air that turns in us. We are not made of music, silence or
elements of their design. The tree that holds the sky and sun
is what the cosmos is, the question and the answer what the birds
in their abandon hear, a tree that in its being tree is where
our speaking starts, our knowledge but the silence that it moves in us,
the words that fall from our mouths the leaves of our invisible.

Finding

Every year the light upon the tree was golden in the late
summer evenings, light that was the sun but separate from the sun
growing in the tree—a larger leaf and something of the tree
that brought it closer to the air of heaven. Every year our eyes
were turned upon the tree filling with light that was not solely of
the sun but its idea in its refulgence, an idea that

minutely in the sun began to grow, a sun in seed that hung
upon the summer air and in the tree, the tree itself in its
idea placed against our eyes, a sun and tree expanding through
the summer that we saw into a sentence whose extensions are
an opening within a sky receding always inward and
without a pause, a sentence that if shaped in words that you or I

might use would be a sentence ramified, where its beginnings graze
upon its endings, an idea that when it is seen is seen
to dance into itself upon the larger heaven of its light—
a tree that is its eschatology in our eyes: *there*
the memory there is of summer, tree, and golden leaf unfolds,
fire in its idea speaking through us speaking the late sun.

We placed our clothes upon the ground. It was an exhalation of
a young moon, its light in fragments falling through the sky, and all
that we might be for others lying here and there upon the grass.
Autumn trees against the sky are no more naked, stripped of their
summer look, the shadows of their branches ghosts among the leaves,
and now we see the shape of us, our history annular upon
our flesh, a place where stars have paused. Touching you, how am I
to know that I am touching you? What other ghosts are there beneath

your flesh my fingers cannot reach, another you that leaps beyond
the air we touch, another flesh invisible, its memories
beyond the grasp of mine? A moon is rising through the trees, the light
suffused, its pale beginnings not in view, the shadow and the light
all that we are given of the trees surrounding us. Were we
to move in circles there, we could not say where trees would end, the dance
that we describe, a dance of trees against a moon, the touch of trees
upon our flesh another breath that we could see within the grass.

Stripped

The pictures in your room are small, succinct as roses, light around
them standing up uncertain what might come descending through the late
summer air. It rests upon my flesh in moments, images
of light that are more punctual than touch, my eyes unable to
contain its passage, stars of light that have no other sky than here,
the space between the door, the walls and window where I am, my eyes
abandoned in their wake—: but stars that flower into flowers of
no shape that I can give, flowers that are what summer is if it

were ours to see, the summer in its ending open, summer in
a room alone, its summerness undressed, beginnings of the grass
laid bare. Whatever summer has, we are of it, intimate
with its unfolded falling. Nothing that the sun keeps hidden is
apart from us unknown. It is not roses that we see, we see
the summer passing through them, deathless summer in the dying rose.
Immortality is naked in your room, its one possession light,
but light inside itself and you and I inside invisible.

Pictures

When we lie down together, we lie down alone without defence
against the planets, passing birds, the dreams of trees that enter us.
The story that we heard of Adam in the garden God had made
is not the story we repeat when we are in our solitude,
no tree dividing us, nor snake. When we lie down together, we
are made of nothing but the dreams that fill our flesh, of stars that rise
within the silence of the body that is ground and garden for
their light; and when they rise, they rise as roses, trees and grass

where animals within the memory of light begin to trace
the movements of their play released from their mythologies as stars
into our flesh, and we are where their knowledge lies alone with us
unspoken and, in moments of our dreams, reborn. We are our flesh
when we awake, but when we lie together through the night, we are
enigmas fleshed: then the lightness of our body knows
of its possession of a genesis, but genesis without
finality, a breath of birth continuous in us and stars.

Together

The shadows that the fences cast grow longer through the brevities
of afternoon until there is but one shadow that spreads across
the ground, the grass invisible as air, and owls everywhere
around us in the turning dark. Our shadows too are now
consumed, and we are shades of that shadow where everything that is
is, the sun unseen, the stoniness that is the moon dissolved:
nothing that is not shadow is within our knowledge, and our flesh,

that is our nearest knowing now is held suspended in the fall
of winter dark, is twilight shaped, the darkness moving through us more
deeply, the moon remembered in the dark of our turning turning
dark, remembered as a bird that we had seen departing, a bird
so small we did not see it as a bird but smallness that was held
in distances of other birds beyond our sight, a smallness now
around us full of shade, a premise of our flesh defining us.

Brevities